SNEAKY PRESS

ISBN 9781922641151

Sneaky Press is the imprint of Sneaky Universe.
www.sneakyuniverse.com
First published in 2021

Sneaky Press
Melbourne, Australia.

The Book
of
Random Car Facts

Sneaky Press

Contents

Random Facts about the Car History

The first car was built by Carl Benz and driven on 31st December, 1879.

In 1998, the last car designed to be started with a hand-crank was released.

While cars had door keys earlier, it wasn't until 1949 that a key was used to start a car.

UK car company British Leyland formed in 1968, was the second largest car company outside the US, behind Volkswagon.

The first mass produced car was the Model T Ford.

In 1909, it took 12 hours to assemble a Model T.

By 1913, thanks to the assembly line, it took only 8 minutes.

55% of all cars on the road in 1916 were Model T Fords.

Ford produced more than 15 million cars between 1909-1927 – that is an average of about 535 000 cars a year.

By the time the last Model T's were produced in 1927, they could be assembled in 24 seconds.

The Model T cost $850 dollars in 1908 (equal to about $25000 in today's money). In 1925, the same car could be bought new for $260 (equal to about $8000 today) as a direct result of car production becoming more efficient. (These costs are in US$ because that is where the cars were produced and bought at the time.)

Holden used to make saddles – yes the thing you put on a horse to ride on it in the 1850s.

Peugeot started making cars in 1890, before that they made hand tools, kitchen equipment and bikes.

Rolls-Royce make plane engines as well as luxury cars.

Toyota makes automatic looms (machines that weave fabric) as well as cars.

In addition to cars, SAAB make military planes, air traffic control systems and radar.

Hyandai also builds ships, engines and other machinery in addition to cars.

Random Facts about Car Production

It is reported that 115 cars are produced each minute, 6875 cars per hour, 165000 per day totalling 60 million cars each year!

25% of all cars produced are made in China.

There are over 30000 unique parts in the average car.

The first four-wheel drive car was produced for the US military in 1940 – It was a Jeep.

Toyota produces 13000 cars each day, making it the largest car producer in the world. Their best selling car is the Corolla, with over 50 million cars sold as of August 2021.

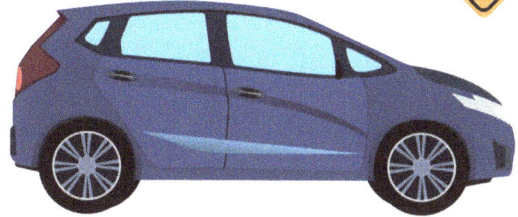

Ford produces 8000-10000 cars are day.

Ferrari produces no more than 14 cars per day

Car Shapes

There are 6 main car shapes.

Hatchback

Coupé

Sedan

 Ute

 Four-wheel drive

 Van

Facts about Car Safety

The day the most car accidents happen is Saturday.

Most accidents happen within 5km of a person's home.

Wearing a seatbelt when riding in a car reduces the risk of death by 61%in an accident.

The three-point seat belt was invented by Volvo in 1959 and saves a life every six seconds. Volvo allowed all other car makers to copy the design so that people could be safer in whatever car they were in.

Airbags were first introduced into some cars in 1974.

It takes 40 milliseconds for an airbag to inflate.

Random Facts about Car Racing

The first car race took place in Paris on July 22, 1894.

Car racing occurs on both public road and race tracks.

Rally racing involves normal cars which have been modified to race.

Only Ford Fusions, Dodge Chargers, Chevrolet Impalas and Toyota Camrys can currently compete in NASCAR races.

Formula 1 racing involves specially designed very fast cars that race laps around a special track.

There are about 15-20 Formula 1 races each year hosted by various countries all over the world. These races combined are called the Grand Prix. The winner of the Grand Prix is the team who has had the most success during the year.

The first formula 1 race occurred on May 13, 1950 in the United Kingdom.

Car Firsts

The first car accident occurred in 1891.

The first road dividing line was painted in Michigan, USA in 1911.

The first traffic lights were installed in 1914 in Cleveland, USA.

The first sign prohibiting left turns was installed in New York, USA in 1916.

Random Car Facts

It is thought that a modern formula 1 car can drive upside down in a tunnel. when moving at the speed of about 190km/h.

Set in November 1985, the record for removing and replacing a car engine is 42 seconds.

The longest car ever made is a Cadillac limousine which was more than 30 meters long and has more than 20 tyres.

The lowest car ever produced is less than 50 cm high – it is called the Flatmobile.

Fancy yourself a singer? It seems most people who drive cars do. 90% of all drivers sing when on the road.

Cars are the most recycled product in the world.

In the United Kingdom, police cars used to have a stash of teddy bears in them just in case officers came across a child who was in a car accident who needed to be calmed down.

There are more Rolls Royces in Hong Kong than anywhere else in the world.

In 2018, approximately 75% of all second-hand cars sold in the United States of America were either Black, white, grey or silver.

In 1981, German car maker Trabant was making cars without fuel gauges. You could check how much fuel you had with a dipstick.

Approximately 65% of motorists around the world drive on the right side of the road.

Wheels have been used a very long time by humans. The oldest one discovered dates back to 3500 BCE. It was found in Mesopotamia.

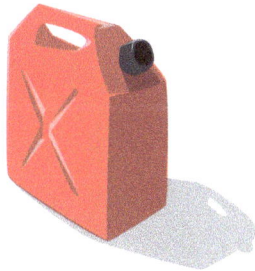

Drivers in Turkmenistan are entitled to 120 litres of free fuel a month.

In Norway, half of all new cars sold are either electric or hybrid.

Leonardo da Vinci designed a car in 1478. The Institute and Museum of History of Science in Florence Italy has a replica of this car which was finally built in 2004.

ROLLS ROYCE

Rolls Royce owners really love and look after their cars – 75% of all Rolls Royces are still on the road.

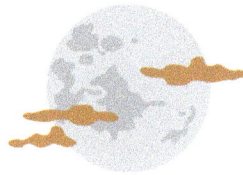

If a car could drive through the air at an average speed of 96 km/h without needing to be refuelled, it would get you to the moon in less than a month.

Many new cars are very quiet, so quiet that they play fake engine noise through the speakers.

In Russia, it is against the law to drive around in a dirty car.

The first speeding ticket was issued in 1902 for a car travelling at about 72km/h.

It used to be against the law to slam a car door in some places in Switzerland.

Car Myths

Horsepower refers to the actual speed of a horse – It is actually just a way to measure how much work is done in a specific amount of time.

Smaller cars are more dangerous for passengers in an accident.

The cost of car insurance depends on the colour of your car.

Old cars are safer.

Dirty cars are more fuel efficient.

Filling up your fuel in the morning gets you better quality fuel.

You need to warm up a car engine in cold weather.

Manual cars are more fuel efficient than automatic cars.

Cars and Language

The modern English word car came into the language from the French "carre". The French word came from the Latin. word for "wheeled vehicle" Carrus.

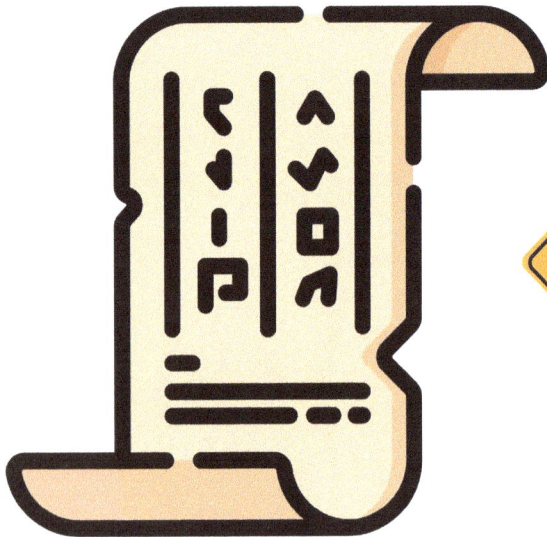

There are many words that refer to having a car accident – prang, fender bender, pile-up, collision, bump, smash, bingle, stack, love tap.

A grease monkey is another name for a mechanic.

There are several words that refer to old cars that are not in great condition: old banger, jalopy, lemon, bomb, wreck, heap, boneshaker, clunker, bucket of bolts, old beater, rust bucket.

Car Idioms

To put the brakes on – to slow something down or to stop.

On a collision course – to be on the path to disaster.

To pick up speed – to start to accelerate at something or something that is accelerating.

START

To hit the road – it is time to leave

To get the show on the road – To start something

Down the road – something is in the future

All roads lead to Rome – it doesn't matter how you do something, the end result will be the same

Shifting gears – means to suddenly change direction

To do a U-turn – to change your mind

Backseat driver – someone who gives unwanted advice to a driver

To be the Driving Force – describes a person who is leading a project or activity

To be driven – means to be motivated

A free ride – to benefit from something without any cost

Car Jokes

What do you call a Spanish man who has lost his car?

Carlos

Who drives their customers away but still makes money?

Taxi drivers

When is a car not a car anymore?

When it turns into a driveway.

What do you call a Ford Fiesta that has run out of fuel?

A Ford Siesta

What did the traffic light say to the car?

Turn away, I'm about to change.

What make of car does a snake drive?

An Ana-Honda

What do you say to a rabbit that needs a ride?

Hop in

What do you get when you put a car and a pet together?

A Carpet

Why are pigs considered bad drivers?

They hog the road.

Car Trivia

1. What is used to inflate car tyres?

2. What are the most common fuels used to power cars?

3. Which car types are often used as work vehicles?

Answers

1. Air

2. Petrol, gas. diesel and electricity

3. Vans and Utes

4. Adding things like spoilers and sunroofs, the colour of the car, what the seats are made of.

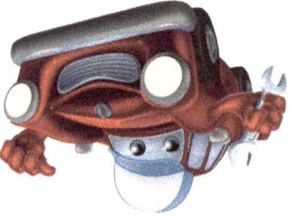

4. What are some changes you can make to cars?

Other titles in the
Random Facts Series

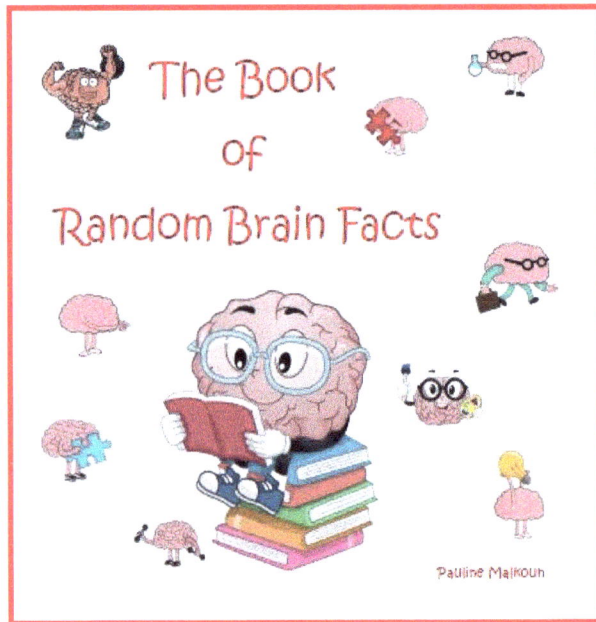

The Book
of
Random Brain Facts

Pauline Malkoun

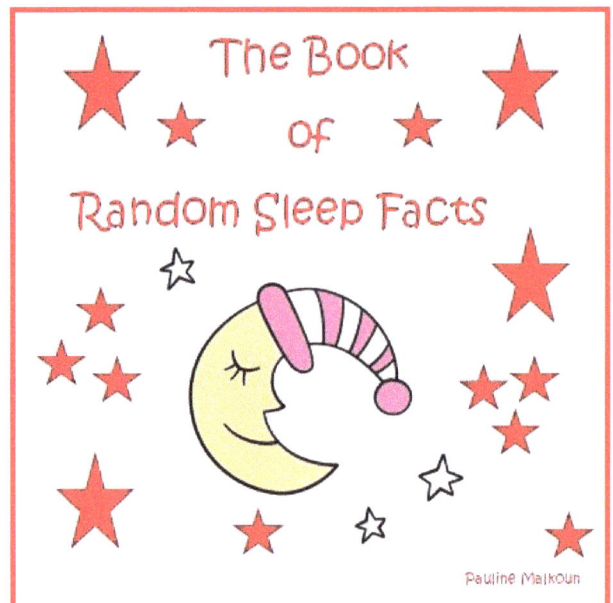

The Book
of
Random Sleep Facts

Pauline Malkoun

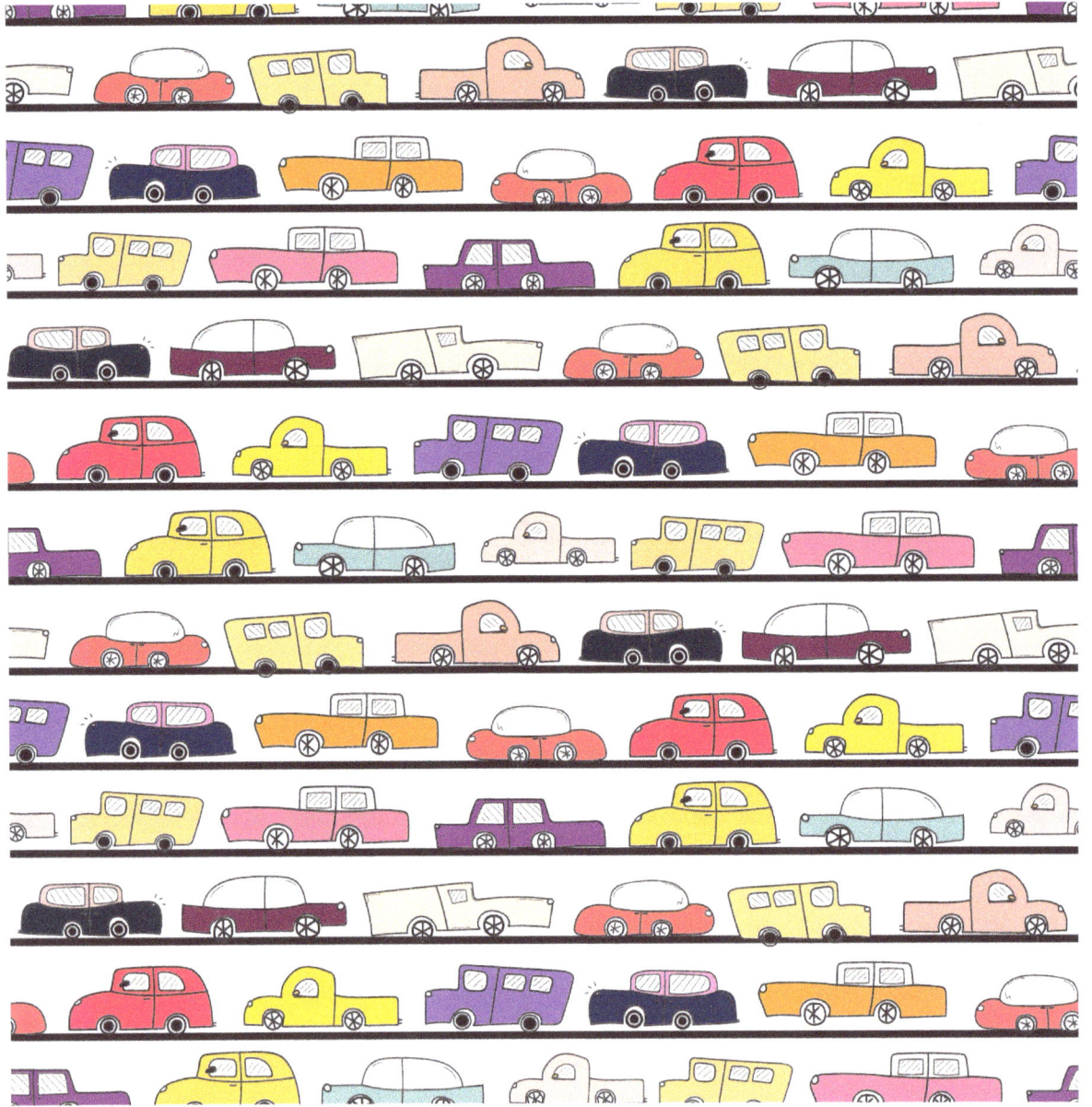